T0132057

OUR GREATEST JURNEE

SELF –AFFIRMATIONS

Written by Nicole &
Jurnee Holness

Illustrated by
Jeressa Whitner

AuthorHouse™
1663 Liberty Drive
Bloomington, IN 47403
www.authorhouse.com
Phone: 1 (800) 839-8640

Because of the dynamic nature of the Internet, any web addresses or
links contained in this book may have changed since publication and may
no longer be valid. The views expressed in this work are solely those
of the author and do not necessarily reflect the views of the publisher,
and the publisher hereby disclaims any responsibility for them.

Any people depicted in stock imagery provided by Getty Images are models,
and such images are being used for illustrative purposes only.
Certain stock imagery © Getty Images.

Illustrated by: Jeressa Whitner

ISBN: 978-1-7283-2119-6 (sc)
ISBN: 978-1-7283-2120-2 (hc)
ISBN: 978-1-7283-2118-9 (e)

Library of Congress Control Number: 2019910654

Print information available on the last page.

This book is printed on acid-free paper.

Published by AuthorHouse 07/29/2019

authorHOUSE®

OUR GREATEST JURNEE

SELF-AFFIRMATIONS

Written by: Nicole & Jurnee Holness
Illustrated by: Jeressa Whitner

I am smart. I am capable.

I am kind.

I am beautiful. I see the beauty in others.

I am brave.

I am confident. I am humble.

I am loving. I am loved.

I am me. I am enough.

Printed in the United States
By Bookmasters